Dancing
to
Freedom

THE TRUE STORY OF
MAO'S LAST DANCER

Li Cunxin   Illustrated by Anne Spudvilas

Walker & Company  New York

First published in Australia in 2007 by Penguin Group (Australia), a division of Pearson Australia Group Pty. Ltd.
Published in the United States of America in 2008 by Walker Publishing Company, Inc.
Distributed to the trade by Macmillan

For information about permission to reproduce selections from this book, write to
Permissions, Walker & Company, 175 Fifth Avenue, New York, New York 10010

Library of Congress Cataloging-in-Publication Data
Li, Cunxin.
Dancing to freedom : the true story of Mao's last dancer / Li Cunxin ; illustrated by Anne Spudvilas.
    p.   cm.
ISBN-13: 978-0-8027-9777-3 • ISBN-10: 0-8027-9777-6 (hardcover)
ISBN-13: 978-0-8027-9778-0 • ISBN-10: 0-8027-9778-4 (reinforced)
1. Li, Cunxin, 1961—Juvenile literature. 2. Ballet dancers—China—Biography—Juvenile literature.
3. Defectors—China—Biography—Juvenile literature. I. Spudvilas, Anne, ill. II. Title.
GV1785.L475A3 2008   792.802'8092—dc22 [B]   2007037150

Visit Walker & Company's Web site at www.walkeryoungreaders.com

Typeset in Codex
The paintings in this book were done in traditional Chinese ink and watercolor on rice paper, and oil paints on canvas

Printed in China
(hardcover) 10 9 8 7 6 5 4 3 2 1
(reinforced) 10 9 8 7 6 5 4 3 2 1

For Sophie, Tom, and Bridie,
May you live your dreams —L. C.

For Tony, my friend in Beijing —A. S.

Some time ago, in a remote village in
northern China, a small peasant boy
lived with his parents and six brothers
in a tiny brick house. They were very poor.

On the bleak farming lands around his village,
the boy would often fly a homemade kite.
It was a gift from his beloved father.

That small boy was me, and my story begins with that kite. On one
bitterly cold day, near our home in Qingdao, I tied some "paper wishes"
to my kite, and my father helped me fly it up into the sky. The kite soared
like a bird, and my hopes and wishes went with it.

Then he sat down beside me, as he always did, and told me a story. I loved all his stories but my favorite one was this . . .

Once upon a time, a little frog lived in a deep, dark well. It was his only home. One day, he met a frog from the world above.

"Come down and play with me!" begged the frog in the well.

The frog from the world above laughed. "My world up here is much bigger!"

The frog in the well was very annoyed, so he told his father what he'd heard.

"My son," his father said with a sad heart, "I have heard there is a bigger and better world up there. But our life is here, in the well. There is no way we can get out."

"I want to see what is out there!" cried the little frog. But even though he jumped and hopped, the well was just too deep.

"It is no use, my son," said his father. "I have tried all my life to get out."

Still, the little frog kept on trying to escape from that deep, dark well . . .

Long after my father had finished his tale,
I kept thinking about that sad little frog in the well.

Back at our house, I would help my mother cook. It was our special time together. When we all sat down to eat, we would stare longingly at what little food there was. Every night our mother would pray that none of her sons would die from starvation.

I was always hungry. At night we slept head to toe, crammed on a hard bed. I hated my brothers' feet in my face.

Still, I would dream about my kite, and the little frog in the well.

And my brothers and I were luckier than some in our village. We survived.

At the age of nine we started school. In winter it was a long, cold walk to our simple schoolroom of mud and straw. The icy winds blew snow through our clothes, chilling us deep in our bones.

One very cold day, four strange officials came into our classroom. They wanted to take some children to study something called ballet. Only one girl was chosen. Then, just as they were about to leave, Teacher Song suddenly pointed at me. "What about this one?" she said.

The girl and I were measured and tested. My legs were lifted high and my body was stretched, but I did not cry out in pain. I thought again of the little frog in the well. Perhaps if I could pass this test I could help my family live a better life.

For many weeks I waited. Then, no one could believe the news! Li Cunxin, a poor peasant boy, had been chosen from the millions of children in the whole of China. I was to leave home and become a dancer.

"Mother," I said, "can you come with me?"

"My dear son," she replied, "this is your one chance to escape this cruel world. You have your secret dreams. Follow them! Make them come true."

I could feel my mother's love as she held me tight in her arms.

And so I waved good-bye to the only home I had ever known. I was just eleven years old.

I was taken away on a crowded train. Such strange sights and sounds at the enormous Beijing Station! I was lost in this vast, teeming city—and all I felt was fear.

Before I knew it, my new life had begun.
I was plunged into my first days at the Beijing
Dance Academy. They were long and hard
and bewildering. I was one of the worst
students, and I felt so shy, lost in an ocean
of loneliness. I missed my mother, and every
night I sobbed myself to sleep.

Sometimes I would find a place to hide among the weeping willows.
The dripping leaves quivered as my tears fell, as if the trees themselves
understood my sadness.

Two years went by before I found a friend. He was called The Bandit,
and we helped each other through. And later I met Teacher Xiao.
Teacher Xiao showed me the most beautiful leaps—graceful as a pheasant,
powerful as a dragon. "Nothing is impossible!" he urged, and he told me
the story of the bow shooter, who had to practice over and over if he
wanted to become the best in all of China.

I loved the stories Teacher Xiao told me. They were stories of courage, hope, and great achievement. So I too began to practice, night after night, turning and turning by the light of a single dim candle.

I practiced for years in those ballet studios. By the time I was eighteen,
Teacher Xiao told me I had become one of the best dancers in China.
I wished so much that my parents could come and see me, but how
would that ever be possible when they were so poor?

Then one day, a famous ballet master came to visit our academy.
His name was Ben, and he asked me if I would like to study ballet in his
country—America. I thought again of the little frog, and I said yes.

Soon I found myself on a plane, traveling halfway across the world. Now I was even farther from my family. I landed in a foreign city of huge highways and enormous buildings. I could not believe what I was seeing! It was not a bit like China.

In America I worked hard on my ballet,
and by the time I was twenty-one I was traveling
all over the world and dancing in great cities like London,
Paris, and Moscow. I had become a star!

But every day I remembered my mother and father, and how lonely life
was without them. It had been many long years since we'd been separated,
and something was always missing in my heart.

One day a wonderful thing happened. I learned that my parents could come from China to see me dance! Could it be true that after all this time I was to see them again?

It was the grand opening of *The Nutcracker*. In the dressing room I looked at my parents' precious photograph, as I always did. Soon I would see their faces, really see them, not just on a piece of paper. My hands were trembling. My heart was beating fast.

At last it was time to dance, and I leaped onto the stage.

Suddenly, through a beam of light . . .

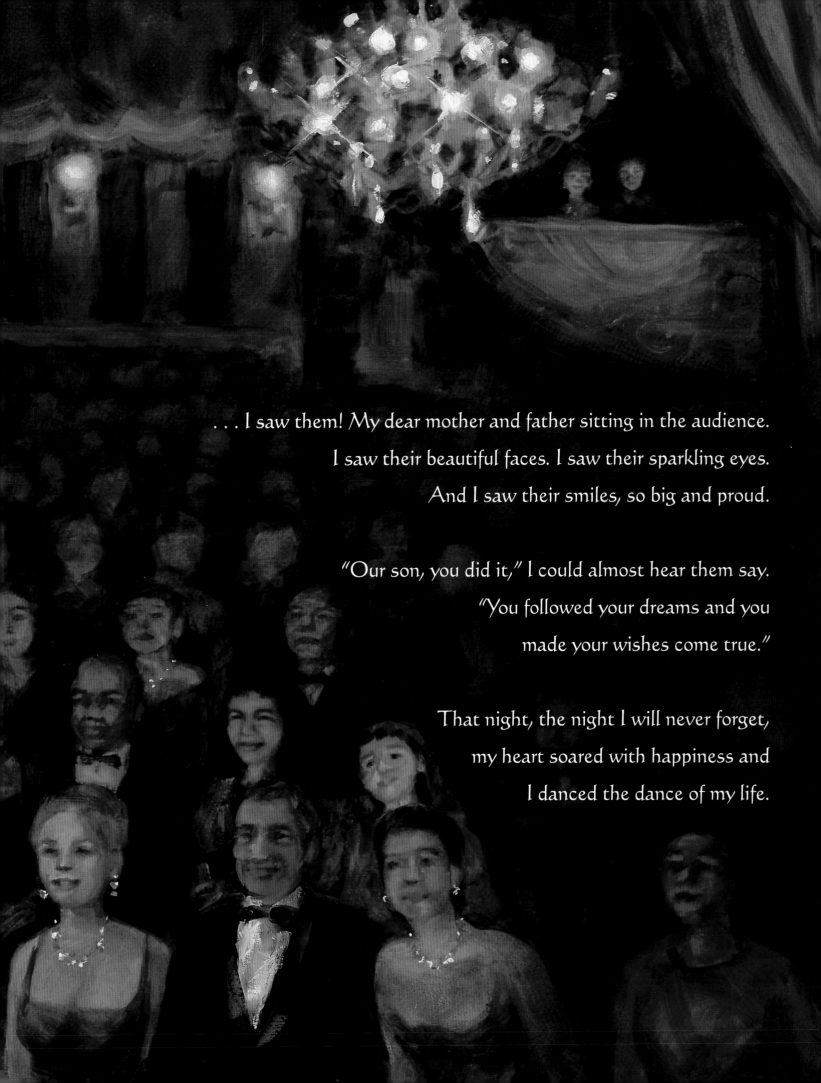

. . . I saw them! My dear mother and father sitting in the audience.
I saw their beautiful faces. I saw their sparkling eyes.
And I saw their smiles, so big and proud.

"Our son, you did it," I could almost hear them say.
"You followed your dreams and you
made your wishes come true."

That night, the night I will never forget,
my heart soared with happiness and
I danced the dance of my life.

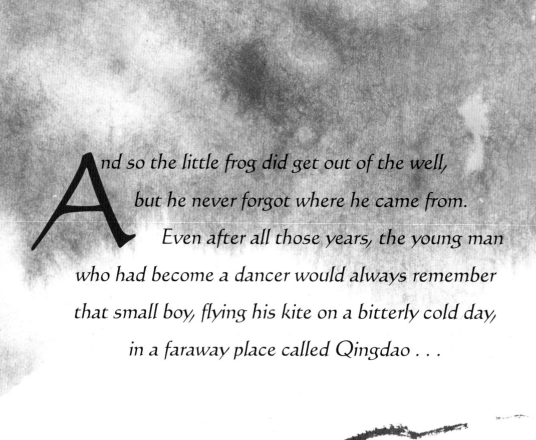

And so the little frog did get out of the well,
but he never forgot where he came from.
Even after all those years, the young man
who had become a dancer would always remember
that small boy, flying his kite on a bitterly cold day,
in a faraway place called Qingdao . . .

ABOUT LI'S CHINA

When this story began, in the 1960s, China's leader was a man named Mao
Zedong. He was chairman of the Communist Party, which started the
Cultural Revolution by organizing China in a very strict way so that
everything people had—their houses, their furniture, their clothes, their
animals—belonged to the government. The government made all the
decisions about how people lived, what they did, what they could own,
and where they could go.

But during this time, many villagers like Li did not have enough food.
They were very poor because the government's ideas about how to run
the country were not working. Millions of people were dying of starvation.

When children were lucky enough to go to school, they had to learn all
about Chairman Mao and show support for him in everything they did.
China was a very difficult country to visit then, or to leave if you lived
there. That is why it was so wonderful for Li's parents to be allowed out of
China to see Li dance. And that is why it was so wonderful for Li to go to
America—a country that most Chinese people at that time were not
allowed to visit or even speak about.

Today, China is a very different place. You can visit exciting places like
Beijing, where Li studied ballet, or the Great Wall of China. Li's parents
still live in Qingdao, but now Li and his family can visit them every year.
Perhaps one day you will visit China too, and remember Li and his family—
and how one thin thread of a chance changed all of their lives.